3 4028 09609 6210
HARRIS COUNTY PUBLIC LIBRARY

Makers as
INNOVATORS
JUNIOR

Coding with Blockly

By Amber Lovett

CHERRY LAKE Publishing

Published in the United States of America by
Cherry Lake Publishing
Ann Arbor, Michigan
www.cherrylakepublishing.com

Series Adviser: Kristin Fontichiaro
Reading Adviser: Marla Conn, MS, Ed., Literacy specialist,
Read-Ability, Inc.
Photo Credits: All images by Amber Lovett

Library of Congress Cataloging-in-Publication Data
Names: Lovett, Amber, author.
Title: Coding with Blockly / by Amber Lovett.
Other titles: 21st century skills innovation library. Makers as innovators.
Description: Ann Arbor, Michigan : Cherry Lake Publishing, [2017] | Series: Makers as
  innovators junior | Series: 21st century skills innovation library | Audience: K to
  grade 3. | Includes bibliographical references and index.
Identifiers: LCCN 2016032412| ISBN 9781634721851 (lib. bdg.) | ISBN 9781634723176
  (pbk.) | ISBN 9781634722513 (pdf) | ISBN 9781634723831 (ebook)
Subjects: LCSH: Computer programming–Juvenile literature. | Programming languages
  (Electronic computers)–Juvenile literature. | Computer graphics–Juvenile literature.
Classification: LCC QA76.52 .L68 2017 | DDC 005.26/2–dc23 LC record available at
  https://lccn.loc.gov/2016032412

Cherry Lake Publishing would like to acknowledge the work of the Partnership for
21st Century Learning. Please visit *www.p21.org* for more information.

Printed in the United States of America
Corporate Graphics

A Note to Adults: Please review the instructions for the activities in this book before allowing children to do them. Be sure to help them with any activities you do not think they can safely complete on their own.

A Note to Kids: Be sure to ask an adult for help with these activities when you need it. Always put your safety first!

Table of Contents

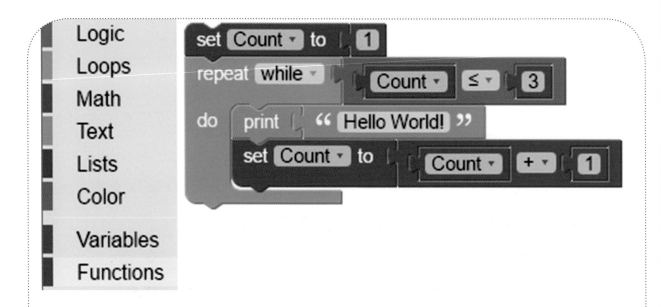

Logic
Loops
Math
Text
Lists
Color

Variables
Functions

```
set Count ▾ to  1
repeat while ▾   Count ▾  ≤ ▾  3
do  print  " Hello World! "
    set Count ▾ to  Count ▾  + ▾  1
```

With Blockly, you can arrange colored blocks to create code.

Learning the Right Words

It might sound like a lot of work to learn a whole new language. Writing code is not easy! But you don't have to be a coding expert to make your first program. You only need to learn enough to be able to move code around.

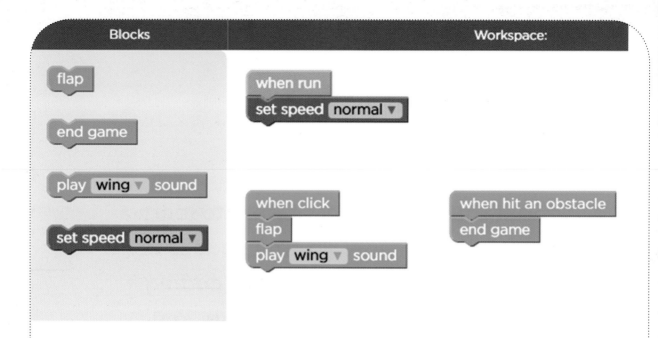

Blocks

flap

end game

play wing ▼ sound

set speed normal ▼

Workspace:

when run
set speed normal ▼

when click
flap
play wing ▼ sound

when hit an obstacle
end game

You can click on code blocks and drag them around. Snap them together to tell the computer what to do.

How Does Blockly Work?

Blockly lets you program without writing code. Instead, you build programs using blocks. It's just like fitting together Lego bricks. The code is hidden inside each block. This makes it a lot easier to create programs.

Practice Makes Perfect

Sometimes your program won't work. You will need to think carefully and look for problems in your work. Don't worry, though. Everyone has trouble learning how to program at first. Practicing is the only way to get better at it.

move forward

turn left ↺ ▾

turn right ↻ ▾

▶ Run Program

If the steps are in the wrong order or missing information, your program won't work. This program will not work because the code needs to say "move forward" after "turn left."

Writing Good Instructions

You might think that computers are smart. It's true that computers are very good at a lot of things. They are especially good at math! But computers can't think on their own. They can only do what they are told. They have to know every single step to follow. And the steps have to be in the correct order.

Try using one of the blocks below:

`move` `forward ▽` `by` `100 ▽` `pixels`

Try again

Sometimes Blockly will give you hints to help you.

Cracking the Code

Let's see if we can crack the code!

```
when click
flap
play  wing ▼  sound
```

Look at this code. It is telling the computer that when we click, we want a bird's wings to flap. Then we want the computer to play the sound of wings flapping.

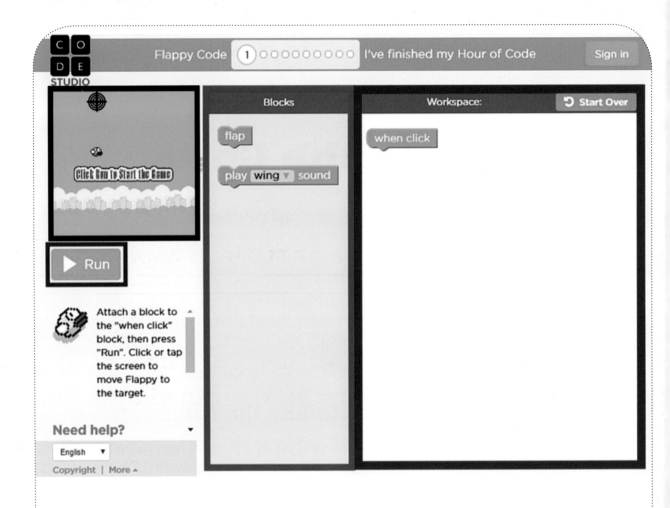

Your screen should look something like this when using Blockly.
This example comes from code.org.

What Does Blockly Look Like?

A lot of Web sites use Blockly. They all look a little different. Let's look at one example.

Blocks

The blue box is where all the blocks live on this Web site. Blocks are often grouped by what they do.

Workspace

Your workspace is where you stack your blocks of code and tell the computer what to do. It is in the red box.

Blocks

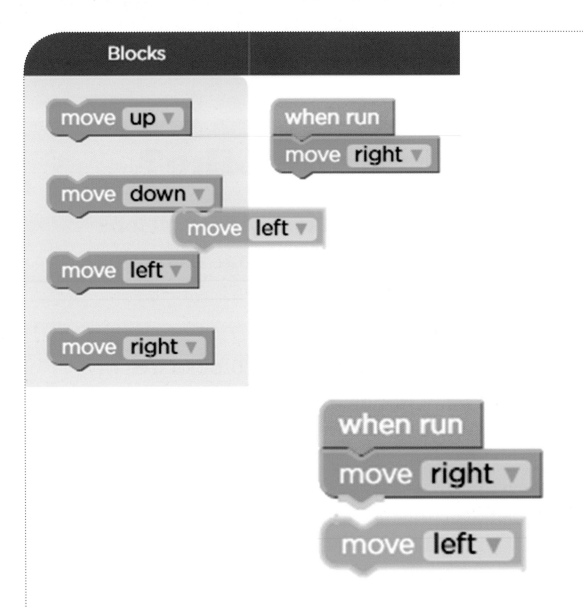

When you see the yellow outline around the box, you can let go of your mouse.

Moving Blocks

Blockly gives you a list of blocks to
use. Click on the block you want. Hold
your finger down. Then drag the block
into the white workspace. Let go of your
mouse to drop the block. It will snap
into place. The computer runs your
program in the order of your blocks.
If you need to move a block, click
and drag it.

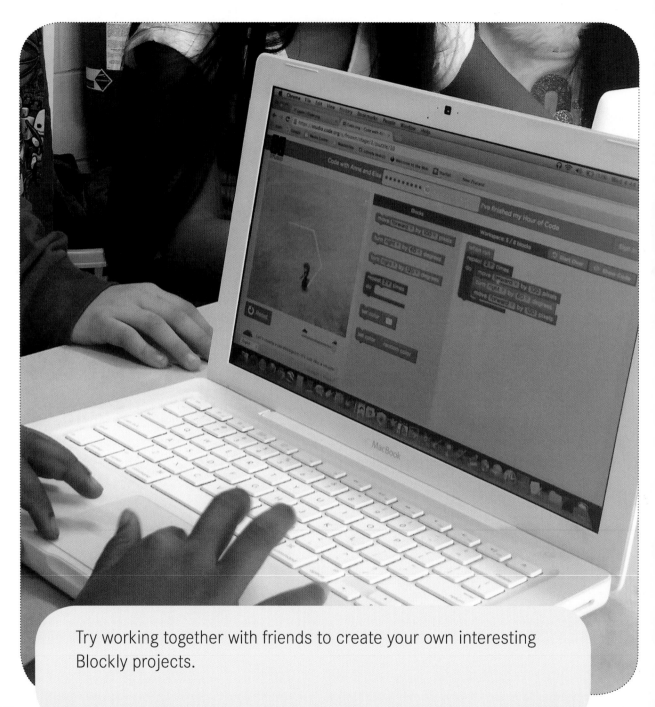

Try working together with friends to create your own interesting Blockly projects.

Adding and Deleting Blocks

You can add as many blocks as you would like. Just remember to think like a computer! Include every step or your program will not work. You can also make your program do two things at once. Just add a new stack of blocks to your workspace.

Getting Rid of Blocks

You can drag blocks you don't want to the trash can. Be careful, though! If you click on the first block in a stack, it will move the whole stack!

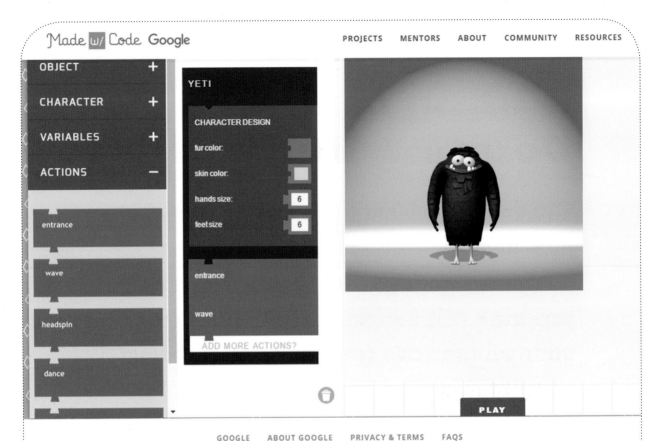

Some Blockly Web sites let you design your own colorful characters. This one comes from Google's madewithcode.com. Using code, you can change what the monster looks like and how it moves.

What If My Code Doesn't Work?

Once you start using Blockly, try clicking the "Run" or "Play" button to test your program. Don't get frustrated if your code doesn't work. Programmers have to fix their code all the time! Remember that the computer isn't as smart as you are. You have to tell it what to do every step of the way.

Now You Try!

Now that you know more about Blockly, it's time for you to try it. Ask an adult to help you visit one of the Web sites listed on page 23. Blockly is even more fun when you have someone to help you!

Glossary

code (KODE) ideas written using a programming language

programming language (PROH-gram-ing LANG-wij) a set of words, symbols, and rules used to write instructions for a computer

symbols (SIM-buhlz) designs or objects that stand for something else

Find Out More

Books

Austic, Greg. *Game Design*. Ann Arbor, MI: Cherry Lake Publishing, 2014.

Benson, Pete. *Scratch*. Ann Arbor, MI: Cherry Lake Publishing, 2016.

Van Lent, Colleen. *Web Design with HTML5*. Ann Arbor, MI: Cherry Lake Publishing, 2015.

Web Sites

Blockly Games
https://blockly-games.appspot.com/
Blockly Games helps you create and play games and puzzles using Blockly.

Code.org
https://code.org
Try using Blockly with Anna and Elsa from *Frozen*, BB-8 from *Star Wars*, and more.

Made with Code
www.madewithcode.com
This Web site from Google has many different Blockly projects that are great for beginners.

Index

About the Author

Amber Lovett likes playing with robots and technology. She teaches science, technology, engineering, and math at a school in Arizona.